And the Sun God Said:

That's Hip

by Ernest Gregg

Pictures by G. Falcon Beazer

Harper & Row, Publishers
New York, Evanston, San Francisco, London

7477

This book is dedicated to our future, our fruits, our nation.

*May they grow
strong*

*May they grow
knowledgeable*

*May they grow
spiritual*

*May they grow
respectful*

*May they grow
to the wisdom
of nation-building.*

I would like to thank K. Willie Kgositsile and Angela Gilliam.

Ernest A. Gregg

The Sun God was lonely...

he had smiled at the trees
blinked to the breeze
whistled for the tides
and made the rain close his eyes.
He had laughed at the moon
and turned darkness into noon.

He gave a party on Mars
and invited all the stars.
He made the animals seek shade
with his rays
and boiled the ocean for a decade.

But the Sun God was still lonely,
as lonely as could be,
cuz he was missin you and me.

Sooo, he decided to have some suns,
I said sons and daughters,
and he called for the water
and told the soil to toil,
sayin:
   Make em like me
   let em reflect my rays.

And you know what?
They obeyed cuz they knew his ways,
but the job wasn't easy
cuz it took one hundred and seven days.

And when it was finished,
the Sun God said:
    That's Hip, they got my head, yeah,
    I see some black, brown, some yellow
    and some red.

And then, he commanded water and soil
to rest their heads.

The Sun God smiled and breathed deep
lookin at everyone each by each
sayin:
   Sun people
   Sun people
   grab a seat cuz we is goin to celebrate
   this happy occasion by havin a feast,
   and after I'se goin to preach.
   I said I'se goin to teach.

So the Sun people ate and cleaned their plates.
And the Sun God said:
   The sermon fo today is called
   Some of Y'all,
and the Sun God began by sayin:

Some of y'all is fat
some of y'all skinny
some of y'all short
and some of y'all tall

Some of y'all are different shades
and some of y'all have different ways,
but y'all Sun people
red, yellow, brown and black,
and that's a fact.

You will reflect my rays
and abide by my ways
and be my light,
now ain't that rat?

And the people said:
    That's Rat!

The Sun God continued:
   Some of y'all heads is goin to be nappy
   some ain't,
   but t'ain't no reason to lose yo head—
   you hears what I said—
   cuz together
   I said,
   together you form a rainbow of black,
   now ain't that a fact?

And the people hollered:
   That's Rat!

And the Sun God rapped on:
   Some of y'all goin to be bright
   some of y'all goin to look near white
   some of y'all is goin to have freckles too, ahuh!
   but don't git uptight, it'll only be a few.

   Some of y'all is goin to be called
   negro, nigra, nigger
   and colored too
   and some of y'all is goin to deny that you is you.

   But y'all is the Sun's rays
   and will reflect my ways
   for if you do that
   y'all truly be black,
   now ain't that a fact?

And the people screamed:
THAT'S RAT!